Thought for the Day

I0103089

By the same author
and published by Rationality Publications

When Time Is at a Premium: Cognitive-Behavioural Approaches to Single-Session Therapy and Very Brief Coaching (2016)

Attitudes in Rational Emotive Behaviour Therapy (REBT): Components, Characteristics and Adversity-Related Consequences (2016)

Windy Dryden Live! (2021)

Windy Dryden Collected! (2022)

The REBT Pocket Companion for Clients, 2nd Edition (with Walter J. Matweychuk) (2022)

The Little Book of Therapeutic Rationality (2022)

'Seven Principles' Series

Seven Principles of Good Mental Health (2021)

Seven Principles of Rational Emotive Behaviour Therapy (2021)

Seven Principles of Single-Session Therapy (2021)

Seven Principles of Doing Live Therapy Demonstrations (2021)

Thought for the Day

A Flexible Approach to
Mental Health

Windy Dryden

Rationality Publications

Rationality Publications
136 Montagu Mansions, London W1U 6LQ

www.rationalitypublications.com
info@rationalitypublications.com

First edition published by Rationality Publications
Copyright (c) 2022 Windy Dryden

The right of Windy Dryden to be identified as the author of
this work has been asserted in accordance with sections 77
and 78 of the Copyright Designs and Patents Act 1988.

A catalogue record of this book is
available from the British Library.

First edition 2022

Condition of sale:
This book is sold subject to the condition that it shall not, by
way of trade or otherwise, be lent, sold or hired out or
otherwise circulated in any form of binding or cover other
than that in which it is published and without a similar
condition including this condition being imposed on the
subsequent purchaser.

ISBN: 978-1-914938-21-4

Preface

This book is made up of 366 thoughts and reflections on the human experience – one for every day of the year. The ideas contained in them display a fairly hard-headed, no-nonsense approach to staying psychologically healthy in an increasingly complex and difficult world. Use this book in any way that is helpful to you and let me know how you get on with putting my ideas into practice (c/o Rationality Publications).

Windy Dryden
London & Eastbourne
July 2022

1

The world is where things happen to us.
The brain is where we process this stuff.

So World x Brain = Response

2

Nobody can control you by pressing your buttons. First, you don't have any buttons, and second, if you did you would be the one pressing them.

3

Life is like a game of cards. It's not so much the cards you are dealt that are important but how you choose to play them.

To think positively about a negative situation is foolish. To think negatively and rigidly about that situation is unhealthy. To think negatively and flexibly about the same situation is wise and healthy.

5

People are frequently preoccupied with knowing that what they experience is normal. They are not so concerned with knowing that their experience is healthy. For normal does not necessarily mean healthy.

6

If you're in two minds, follow the healthy one.

People are reluctant to take responsibility because they confuse responsibility with blame. Responsibility is, 'I did it with my little hatchet, but I am not a bad person for doing so.' This attitude will help you to understand why you acted in the way that you did and help to prevent you acting that way again.

Blame, on the other hand, is, 'I did it with my little hatchet and I am a bad person for doing so.' This attitude will prevent you from understanding the reasons for your behaviour and will therefore not prevent its recurrence.

So, take responsibility for your actions without blaming yourself for them.

8

Don't be afraid to admit that you don't know something. This means that you are a person who does not know something. It does not mean that you are an ignorant person. With this attitude, owning up to your ignorance will spur you to find out the answer to what you don't know.

9

The person who said, 'When you assume, you make an ASS of U and ME' was wrong. It is human to make assumptions. The trick is to treat your assumptions as hypotheses about reality which need to be checked against reality, rather than as unquestionable facts.

10

Experts are worth listening to, but they are not infallible. They also may not know your individual situation. So don't use the thinking of experts as a substitute for your own thinking.

11

Use one of the rules of baseball in life. Try something three times and if it doesn't work, strike out and use a different approach.

You may be able to reach perfection at something, but you cannot maintain it. In 1984, the British figure skaters, Torvill and Dean, achieved a perfect 6.0 for their ice-skating routine at the Winter Olympics. In all probability, however, they wouldn't have done as well if they'd had to skate the same routine again directly afterwards.

When people tell you to 'pull yourself together' they are treating you as if you were a pair of curtains.

14

Be very sceptical of therapists who comment publicly on the lives of famous people. If they have seen such people for counselling, then they are acting unethically, and if they don't know them personally, then they are speaking from ignorance.

15

Don't give other people advice that you are not prepared to take yourself.

16

Pedestals are for statues, not for humans.

Experience always teaches you something, but you don't always learn from experience.

18

Laws may avenge bad behaviour, but they cannot prevent it.

19

Admitting to ignorance is a prerequisite to learning.

20

Do not search for happiness. Rather, commit yourself to pursuing something that is personally meaningful to you, and you might find happiness along the way.

21

You cannot live in the past, but you can waste a lot of time in the present thinking about the past.

It's no good running away from yourself, for wherever you go you take yourself with you.

If there is a planet where justice and fairness exist as a matter of course, it is not called Earth.

24

Failure is much more interesting than success, for you have much more to learn from failure than you do from success.

People who work in the mental health field often don't take lunch hours. And then they have the audacity to run stress management classes.

26

---◆---

If someone gives you advice, don't automatically assume that it is right and don't automatically assume that it is wrong. Evaluate the advice carefully and take it if it makes sense to you.

27

Just because you look up to someone doesn't mean that they are always right. Think critically about what your idols say.

There are two phrases that are characteristic of a healthy, enquiring mind. They are: 'I don't know,' and 'I'll find out.'

29

To admit that you were wrong after being convinced that you were right is a mark of great maturity.

30

People are influenced by what is in their heads, not what is in yours.

31

When you sweep things under the rug they
have a nasty habit of not going away.

32

Think about your problems when you can do something about them. Otherwise, you will remind yourself of your helplessness.

33

All humans are capable of the greatest good and the worst evil.

However, because we cannot accept this, we locate badness in others, thus preserving the myth that we are good.

35

What you learn determines your behaviour far more than what you are taught.

36

A hundred people chanting a falsehood doesn't make it true.

Money won't make you happy, but I'd rather be rich and miserable than poor and miserable.

38

People who tell you that you can do anything you want are giving you dangerous advice if you want to fly.

39

Reaching out to others when you could do with help is a sign of strength, not a sign of weakness.

Thinking for yourself – one of the great gifts of being human.

41

---◆---

Letting others do your thinking for you –
one of the great follies of being human.

It is important that you guard against emotional reasoning, where you believe that something is true because you strongly feel that it is true (e.g. 'Because I strongly feel in my gut that my girlfriend is seeing someone else, therefore she is'). Just because you have a strong feeling, it doesn't follow that this feeling is necessarily a good guide to reality. It may be, but it doesn't have to be, so test your strong feelings against reality.

For a similar reason, it is important to guard against cognitive reasoning, where you are sure that something is true because you think it is true (e.g. 'Because I think that people are following me, this proves that they are'). For obvious reasons, it is important to test such thoughts against reality.

Don't be dazzled by complicated rhetoric. Just because something sounds profound doesn't mean that it is profound.

45

Don't dismiss simple ideas. Just because something sounds simple doesn't mean that it is simplistic.

If you think that you have things perfectly sorted out, then you are deluding yourself or your mind is so closed that it won't let in new information.

———◆———

Be wary of organisations that say they have an award for putting people first. Sometimes, these organisations are likely to put awards before people.

———◆———

The mind may in many respects rule your body, but if you don't look after your body, your mind may end up ruling a ruin.

49

---◆---

How can you tell if what you think you want is really what you want or what others want for you? Imagine that others want you to do the opposite. If you are prepared to change to meet their expectations, your original desire is not what *you* really want.

50

---◆---

If you think that enjoying yourself is a waste of time, then take a long, hard look at your life values.

51

---◆---

Do you feel overwhelmed? Then you probably take on too much in life. It may be useful to ask yourself how, since you are not enjoying the one life that you do have, you are going to enjoy the two (or three) that you are trying to live at the same time.

52

Get yourself a vitally absorbing interest and pursue it actively, but not obsessively. You'll be happier in the long run if you do.

53

If you haven't had at least three good laughs on a particular day, watch a Marx Brothers video (or whatever you find funny) before you go to bed.

Here's a thought for those in the legal profession who are scared of making mistakes. While you can resign from the Law Society, you can't resign from the 'Flaw Society'.

Happiness comes more from striving to achieve a valued goal than from actually achieving it.

Holding flexible attitudes towards life's adversities leads to you experiencing negative but healthy emotions towards these adversities. These healthy emotions may well be very powerful. However, they are still healthy.

Rigid and extreme attitudes are often a feature of great works of literature. *Wuthering Heights* is a good example of this. However, just because such attitudes are dramatic and exciting to read about doesn't mean that you need to hold them in your own life. Unless you want to be miserable, that is.

If you believe that you absolutely have to have something, you will be disturbed if you do have it because you can always lose it. The healthy alternative is to really want something, but showing yourself that you don't absolutely have to have it.

Trying to convince yourself that you don't care about achieving something that you inwardly believe you absolutely must achieve won't work because it is a lie. Rather, convince yourself that you really want to achieve it, but you don't absolutely have to.

60

Whenever you disturb yourself, ask yourself what conditions would have to exist to take your disturbance away. When you have identified these conditions, show yourself that it is your rigid attitudes towards these conditions that are at the core of your disturbance. Examine these rigid attitudes and replace them with flexible attitudes.

61

---◆---

Beware of using words like 'always' and 'never', for they tend to be too limiting. However, do not conclude from this that you should never use the word 'always' or always refrain from using the word 'never'.

Thinking that you must be perfect is an error – which proves that you are not perfect.

63

People often ask me why I write so much. The answer is that I enjoy writing and I don't demand that I must be inspired before I write.

The only productive thing that you can do with past mistakes is to learn from them. Demanding that you absolutely should not have committed these errors in the first place can impede the learning process.

65

Just because something is new doesn't mean that it is better than the old.

Give people the right to be wrong. They will exercise this right whether you give it to them or not.

67

Have you noticed how rigid and extreme popular songs and lyrics can be? You can practise becoming more flexible and non-extreme by rewriting these titles and lyrics. Here's a few to be going on with:

- You're someone even though nobody loves you.
- I can still live (and be happy) if living is without you.
- I don't have to be-e-e-e-e-e perfect.
- I can stand it, when you touch me.
- I'd like your love so bad, but I don't need it.

Epictetus, the great Roman philosopher, said that people are disturbed not by things. but by the *rigid* and *extreme* attitudes they hold towards things.

69

There is no reason why people must not do the dirty on you, but there is also no reason why you have to put up with it.

Insisting that you must not make mistakes is a mistake in itself. The healthy alternative is to give up the demand that you must not make errors and learn from them when, not if, you make them.

The path to mental health is not taken by reducing your high standards, but by giving up your demands that you must achieve these standards.

If Mozart had consulted me regarding his anxiety about writing his magnum opus, the Requiem Mass, I would not have urged him to give up his plans to write it, nor would I have suggested that he write a few simple sonatas instead. Rather, I would have encouraged him to write his Requiem Mass and to adopt the flexible attitude that while it was important for him to write it, it wasn't an absolute necessity for him to do so.

72

You can ruin even the best of ideas by becoming dogmatic about it.

———————◆———————

When a misfortune happens to you it is quite natural for you to exclaim, 'Why me!?' This is often a rhetorical question which *really* means: 'It absolutely should not have happened to me.' Instead ask, 'Why NOT me?' You will see that there are no good reasons why you should be absolutely immune from such misfortune.

Acknowledging this does not mean that you should not have healthy bad feelings about what has befallen you.

When you demand that others must act in a certain way, you are depriving them of their free choice.

When you are with others, demanding that you must say something interesting before you speak will lead you to stay silent.

You are special to yourself, but you are not special in the universe. So, if you think that the universe has to give you what you want because you are special, you are in for a rude awakening.

—◆—

When you make demands, you are in danger of neglecting your physical and mental health since your demands will drive you on at times when it is healthy for you to stop.

A major obstacle to emotional growth is dogmatism. But take care, for you can be dogmatic about not being dogmatic.

If something happened, it empirically should have happened, for all the conditions were in place for it to happen. For this reason, it makes no sense to demand that what happened absolutely should not have happened. So don't waste time making such demands; rather, learn from what happened so you can try to avoid it happening again in the future.

We often think that we are immune from certain negative life events. If one such event happens to us, we say something like: 'I didn't think that it would ever happen to me.' But we don't have such immunity, and if we accept this, we will take due care and attention to avoid such events if we can do so and not disturb ourselves if we cannot.

When we demand that we be immune from certain life events and one such event happens to us, we then think that we are highly vulnerable to danger. Our perception of increased vulnerability stems from our unmet demand for immunity.

82

It is healthier to be flexible and wrong than rigid and right.

83

When you hold rigid attitudes towards yourself, you are abusing yourself. Instead, when you hold flexible attitudes towards yourself, you are encouraging yourself.

Almost certainly there is no absolute certainty.

Spend some time at the end of the day reviewing what you did well that day. If you cannot write down at least ten things you may have an unhealthy attitude towards achievement, which is preventing you from recognising what you do well.

Some people don't even listen to their still, small, flexible and non-extreme voice when it is screaming loudly in their ear.

Smokey Robinson's mother used to tell her son when he was young, 'Son, from the day you are born till you ride in the hearse, there's nothing so bad it couldn't be worse.'

Here's to you, Mrs Robinson.

---◆---

Some people are reluctant to 'accept' reality because they believe that acceptance means resignation. It does not. Acceptance really means:

- Acknowledging that an event (normally a negative event) has occurred.
- Evaluating the event as bad.
- Recognising that all the conditions were in place that led to the event occurring.
- Noting that you cannot change these past conditions, but that you may be able to change the conditions that currently exist and if you can, striving determinedly to do so.

Resignation means that you do nothing to try and change what currently exists.

People may also be reluctant to 'accept' reality because they believe that if they accept something obnoxious then they are condoning it. This is wrong. You cannot accept something that you refuse to condone.

People often think that the healthy alternative to awfulising is indifference. It is not. The healthy alternative to awfulising is non-awfulising: acknowledging that a negative event is bad, but not the end of the world. Indifference means regarding something as neither bad nor good. Thus, to be indifferent about something negative is not healthy.

91

If you have an attitude of unbearability towards adversity then you believe that you cannot bear or tolerate it.

Developing an attitude of bearability towards adversity involves showing yourself that:

(i)   it is a struggle to bear the adversity
(ii)   you can bear it
(iii)   it is worth bearing
(iv)   you are worth bearing it for
(v)   you are willing to bear it
(vi)   you are going to bear it.

93

It is not healthy, therefore, to bear what is not worth bearing.

94

---◆---

When you say that you can't do something, do you mean:

(a)   that you are literally unable to do it,
(b)   that you are able to do it, but you don't want to, or
(c)   that you have the ability to do it but not the skills?

'Can't' applies only to the first scenario, not the other two.

95

We often settle for chronic discomfort to avoid acute discomfort. We do so because we think, wrongly, that we cannot bear to experience the acute discomfort. However, if we are prepared to bear the acute discomfort and see that it is in our interests to do so, then we will increase our chances of escaping from chronic discomfort.

96

Discomfort is uncomfortable. It's not supposed to be anything else. Put up with it only if it is in your healthy interests to do so.

Being able to bear confusion is the first step to becoming unconfused.

Do you believe that you are unlovable? The problem lies in your relationship with yourself, not in others' opinion of you. Once you have begun to accept yourself as a fallible human being with a mixture of good, bad and neutral points, you will begin to acknowledge that others can find you lovable.

———◗◆◖———

When you condemn yourself for something, ask yourself whether or not you would condemn your best friend for the very same thing. If not, why not treat yourself as your own best friend?

100

Are you afraid of making a fool of yourself? Well, I've got good news for you. You can't do it. Certainly you can do something foolish, but that just proves that you are a fallible human being who can act foolishly.

If you were a fool, all you could do in life would be to act foolishly. It would only take one non-foolish act to prove that you weren't a fool. Reading this book is just such an act!

Since you're not a fool, you can't make a fool of yourself.

101

Nobody can make you feel inadequate without your agreement that you are inadequate.

102

———◆———

Sticks and stones may break your bones, but names can never hurt you. Unless you apply them to yourself.

103

If someone rejects you, they may be saying more about their desires than about you. However, they may be giving you valuable feedback about an aspect of you that may turn off other people too. If you let go of the attitude that being rejected means that you are a rotten person, you will be able to think objectively about which of these two possibilities best explains the rejection.

When asked what I do for a living, I often unthinkingly say that I am a psychologist. It's the 'I am' bit that is the problem here, for it points to my identity, whereas 'psychologist' is only one of a large number of roles that I perform in life. So, to emphasise my complexity as a human being and when I have my wits about me, when asked what I do for a living I will reply: I work as a psychologist.

105

When you compare yourself to another, make sure that the comparison is focused on something specific and tangible, like a skill, for example. Doing so will enable you to learn from the comparison if you discover that the other person is better at the skill than you are.

106

By contrast, when you compare yourself to another, don't focus on your 'self' and the 'self' of the other. Otherwise, you might wrongly conclude that the other person is better than you, not only at the skill but as a person.

107

Don't try to improve yourself, because you just can't do it. You can improve specific things about you but your whole self is far too complex to be improved.

108

---◗◆◖---

If you are reading this in a room, take a look around you and try to give the room one global rating, that completely accounts for it in all its complexity/ You can't do it, can you? Why not? Because the room is too complex to be given a single rating. So, if you can't rate a room, how can you rate a human being who, after all, is far more complex than a room?

The answer is that you can't – at least legitimately.

This is one reason why the concept of self-esteem is problematic. For it involves you giving your 'self' a single rating (or estimation) that completely accounts for it, which, of course, cannot be legitimately done.

110

---◆---

So, what is the healthy alternative to self-esteem? The answer is unconditional self-acceptance. When you accept yourself without conditions, you acknowledge that you are a complex, unique, fallible human being who cannot be given a single rating, but whose specific aspects can be rated.

111

But what if you want to continue esteeming yourself? How can you do this without getting into emotional trouble? The only way to do this is to make your self-esteem unconditional. Show yourself that you are worthwhile, for example, because you are alive, fallible and unique – conditions which will not change in your lifetime. Of course, this does entail making a leap of faith, for you could equally argue that you are worthless because you are alive, fallible and unique. But if you are prepared to make this leap and apply unconditional self-esteem consistently it will help you.

112

The real problem with self-esteem, then, is when it is used conditionally, e.g. I am worthwhile if… (I am successful, I am loved, I do well at work, etc.). If you place conditions on your self-esteem, you will be emotionally disturbed if these conditions aren't met, and you will be vulnerable to emotional disturbance when the conditions are met because they can always be unmet again.

113

Do not attach a label to yourself since it is too limiting and may prevent you from changing. I used to think of myself as a stammerer and this label prevented me from speaking more fluently. It was also untrue, for even when my stammer was at its worst, I spoke fluently more often than I stammered.

Are you scared of rejection? If you are it may come as a surprise to you to learn that you probably are more scared of self-rejection than you are of being rejected by others. For if you accepted yourself in the face of rejection by others, would you still be scared of rejection?

115

Are you too proud to admit that you are wrong? This is not pride, it is a refusal to accept your humanity. By all means be proud, but be proud of being human. This will help you to admit your mistakes and to move forward.

116

You are no better than anyone else. But you are no worse, either.

117

Make 'fallible' the only adjective you use to describe yourself and others.

118

You are not a good person, but parts of you
are good.

119

You are not a bad person, but parts of you are bad.

120

You are not an average person, but parts of you are average.

121

So who are you? You are a unique mixture of the good, the bad and the average.

122

You are unique. There will never be another you. Even if we cloned you, you and your clone would be different because you would have different experiences.

123

You are unique. Just like everybody else.

124

Do you think you are stupid? If you really were a stupid person, stupidity would be your essence. This would mean that the only things you could do in life would be stupid things. This is hardly likely. In reality you are not a stupid person, you are a fallible human being who is capable of acting stupidly and non-stupidly.

125

You are not a boring person. But you do have the capacity to bore some people and interest others.

126

If you really were unlovable, this would mean that nobody would be able to love you. This is hardly likely. The truth is that you are both lovable and unlovable, meaning that some people will be able to love you and others won't. Do you know anyone who is either lovable or unlovable?

127

If you find it difficult to accept compliments, realise that in doing so you are negating the feelings of those who compliment you.

From one perspective, if you find it difficult to accept compliments, you can be said to be arrogant. Thus, when you respond to a compliment by saying something like, 'No, it was nothing, really,' you are implying that you are so great that what you are complimented for is commonplace for you.

129

From another perspective, of course, if you find it difficult to accept compliments then you believe that you do not deserve to be complimented.

130

There are no winners and losers in life. There are only people who win and lose at certain things. So don't label yourself or other people on the basis of wins and losses.

131

Would you build a house without strong foundations? Of course not. Then why build a life without recognising and honouring your own strengths?

Do you ever think that you are not good enough? Who aren't you good enough for? If you consider carefully you will realise that that person is you.

133

If you truly accept yourself, warts and all, you will surely think that you are not good enough.

134

If you haven't made any mistakes lately, you are either dead or playing things extraordinarily safely.

135

When you think you are worthless, you act as if you are worthless. Others may then treat you as though you are worthless, which reinforces your idea that you are worthless.

136

'Who am I?' is an unanswerable question. Questions such as 'What do I value?' and 'What are my qualities?' are answerable. So, stop asking yourself who you are.

137

Showing yourself compassion means treating yourself as you would a best friend.

138

Refusing to ask for help when you could do with it is a sign of weakness, not a sign of strength. It shows that you consider yourself to be a weak person if you ask for help.

139

Trying to gain the approval of everyone you meet because you believe that you must have their approval is the best way of losing touch with yourself.

140

So, give up the need for approval. Wanting approval, but realising that you don't need it, will help you to be yourself.

141

Are you a perfectionist? If you ever reached perfection it would mean that you would be incapable of making a mistake and you would have nothing else to learn. Since making mistakes and continuing to learn are two fundamental qualities of being human, striving for perfection means striving to be inhuman.

142

---◆---

There are two types of anger: unhealthy anger and healthy anger. Unhealthy anger stems from the idea that what you are angry about absolutely should not exist, while healthy anger stems from the idea that it would be desirable if it didn't exist but there is no reason why it must not exist.

143

To say that someone made you angry is to give them power over your brain. In reality, you make yourself angry over the other person's behaviour by your anger-creating attitudes.

Where do these attitudes reside? In your brain.

Who is largely in control over your brain? You are.

So don't be too quick to hand over this power of control to someone else.

Procrustes was an innkeeper who held the rigid attitude that his guests had to have a good night's sleep. Holding this attitude and only having one size of bed, he cut off the legs of guests who were too tall for the bed, and stretched the guests who were too short for it.

When you are unhealthily angry, you have a similar philosophy to Procrustes. You believe that events must match your conception of how things must be and, consequently, you try angrily to make them fit your Procrustean bed.

The healthy alternative to this is develop a flexible attitude whereby you acknowledge that it would be nice if things were as you want them to be, but they don't have to fit your size bed.

It was alleged that Voltaire, the French author once said to someone: 'I disapprove of what you say but I will defend to the death your right to say it.' This is a good example of healthy anger. If he had said: 'I disapprove of what you say and you have no right to say it,' he would have experienced unhealthy anger.

146

Every time you blame others you make it more likely that you will blame yourself in the future.

147

If you really understand someone from their point of view, it is difficult to resent them.

148

We do not question the idea that our enemies are bad, but we do object long and loud when our enemies consider us to be bad.

149

Anger without condemnation is healthy.

150

---◆---

Martin Luther King and Gandhi are good role models for healthy anger. Both were angry about injustice and both were persistent in their ongoing attempts to right wrongs. But neither advocated violence and both showed that they respected themselves and others.

When anger leads to considered, constructive action, it is healthy. When it leads to impulsive, unconstructive action, it is unhealthy.

Are you scared of losing control if you express anger? If so, you probably hold one or both of the following two rigid attitudes: (1) I must be in control at all times, and (2) I mustn't feel angry.

153

Once you learn that there is no prohibition on feeling angry and that you don't always have to be in control, then you won't fear losing control while expressing anger and your anger expression is likely to be focused and respectful, but clear.

154

—◆—

When you experience unhealthy anger, it is worth asking yourself if it is a cover for feelings of hurt, shame or anxiety, for example.

155

If your unhealthy anger is a cover for another unhealthy negative emotion, accept yourself unconditionally for feeling anger and the other emotion and then ask yourself what you feel most disturbed about.

156

Unhealthy anger and its associated behaviours can be an attempt to destroy something or someone that you find very threatening.

Sometimes, however, unhealthy anger is just plain unhealthy anger.

158

Some forms of unhealthy anger are examples of two-year-old-ism, where you have an attitude: 'Because I want something, I absolutely have to have it and you have to give it to me.'

159

Other forms of unhealthy anger serve to protect you from threats to your self-esteem. It is as if you are saying: 'You must not remind me how worthless I think I am.'

160

It is popularly believed that when you feel angry, it is important to let it out. I disagree. When your anger is unhealthy and you let it out, you do two things. First, you practise the rigid attitude that underpins your anger, and second, you may well do harm to the person to whom you express your unhealthy anger.

161

King Canute was unhealthily angry when he demanded that the tide went out on his command. His anger had no effect on the tide and his feet got wet.

162

There are basically two types of anxiety: discomfort anxiety (DA) and ego anxiety (EA). Anxiety arises when you hold rigid and extreme attitudes towards threats to your sense of comfort (DA) or to your self-esteem (EA).

163

Discomfort anxiety stems from the rigid attitude that conditions in your life must not be uncomfortable and it is terrible if they are.

Ego anxiety stems from the rigid attitude that you must do well and/or be approved and that you are worthless if you do poorly or are disapproved.

165

When you feel anxious you will experience a strong tendency to withdraw from the threat or avoid situations where it may occur.

166

---◆---

Withdrawal and avoidance lead to the perpetuation of anxiety. Why? Because every time you withdraw from or avoid a threatening situation, you rehearse and thereby strengthen the rigid and extreme attitudes that underpin your anxiety and you deprive yourself of the experience of dealing with the threat should it come to pass.

167

If you can't withdraw from or avoid the threat, you may find yourself trying to distract yourself from it. People think that it is good to distract yourself from threat because it lowers your anxiety. This may happen, but distraction is only helpful in the very short term. Its use often prevents you (1) from facing the threat fair and square and dealing with it and (2) from identifying, examining and changing the rigid and extreme attitudes that largely determine your anxiety.

Are you anxious? Do you demand guarantees in life? The only guarantee that I will give you is this: I guarantee that you will remain anxious as long as you demand a guarantee. The healthy alternative is to acknowledge that while you might want a guarantee, you don't need one. Once you hold this flexible attitude, you will see much more clearly that such guarantees do not exist.

169

The next time someone tells you not to worry, ask them for precise instructions of how you can do this.

---◆---

Feelings of anxiety lead to an exaggeration of threat which may well, in turn, result in increased anxiety.

171

If you try desperately to control your anxiety, you will only succeed in increasing your anxiety. The problem here is your desperation. Thus, if you want to control your anxiety, do so without desperation.

172

Anxiety can be a very painful feeling, but it is not an 'end of the world' experience. If you regard it as such you will transform your anxiety into panic. So, if you don't want to panic, take the horror out of anxiety.

173

---◆---

The healthy alternative to anxiety is concern, not calmness. If you are faced with a threat, you want to be mobilised to deal with it. Concern will help you to do this; calmness won't.

174

---◆---

It is good to be in control, but if you demand that you must be in control you will be anxious when you begin to lose control. Also, demanding that you must be in control will lead you to overestimate the degree to which you will lose control. Thus, people who hold rigid attitudes towards self-control think that they are either in control or totally out of control. They envisage themselves falling apart or ending up a gibbering wreck in a psychiatric hospital.

However, if you hold a flexible attitude towards self-control whereby you want to be in control, but this is not a necessity, then you will see that control lies on a continuum and is not an either/or experience. Thus, if you begin to lose control you will be concerned about this, but not frightened by it. This attitude will help you to regain control.

People often try to relax when they are anxious. This is not necessarily a bad idea, but use relaxation techniques after you have identified, examined and changed your anxiety-creating attitudes. If you try to relax without first changing these attitudes, you may help yourself on this one occasion, but you will render yourself vulnerable to anxiety in the future because your anxiety-creating attitudes remain intact.

176

If there is anything certain in the universe it is that there is no certainty. Yet innumerable people demand certainty. A common example of this is the demand to know instantly that an unexplained symptom is benign. People who make such a demand come to think that a state of uncertainty means that there is something wrong with them. It is only when they give up this demand that they can see that uncertainty is not synonymous with illness. In fact, it is very common to have an unexplained symptom that is benign. This does not mean that we should ignore unexplained symptoms. It is healthy to be concerned and vigilant, and being so will help us to wait and see what happens and to take steps if the symptom does not clear up. However, we can't do this if we demand instant certainty that there is nothing wrong with us. This attitude will lead us to constantly seek reassurance which we cannot believe. This is because when we demand certainty we are not reassurable.

When you are anxious you not only overestimate the degree of threat you are facing, you also underestimate your ability to cope with the threat. So, after you have identified, examined and changed the attitudes that are at the core of your anxiety, develop a list of your coping resources and regularly put these resources into practice until you have increased your confidence in your ability to cope.

Courage is taking constructive action even though you feel afraid.

179

If you consider that you can stop something from happening by worrying about it, you are deluding yourself and seducing yourself into a lifetime of worry.

180

---◆---

Security resides in an attitude that you take towards something. It does not reside in possessing the thing itself. For even if you possess something that you think makes you secure, you could always lose it. But if you want it, but don't need it, then you are secure whether you have it or not.

181

Nobody is afraid of flying. You may be afraid that the plane may crash or that you may lose control or you may be uncertain about what is going to happen to you. But nobody has ever said: 'Oh my God, the plane that I am going on might fly.'

———◆———

Do you think that you need a guarantee that everything will turn out for the best? Yes? OK, then here it is: I guarantee that everything will turn out for the best. Happy now? No? Then perhaps the problem is in your attitude that you need a guarantee.

183

If you want to stop worrying, strive to take the horror, but not the badness, out of everything. But realise that you cannot do this perfectly once and for all. It is a process, not an outcome.

When you worry you frequently ask yourself 'what if...' questions. When you do so, assume that the 'what if?' will happen and do two things: (1) take the horror out of it, and (2) prove to yourself that you can deal with it even though it will probably be difficult.

185

People who worry are like readers of a novel who close the book at the scary bits. To stop worrying go through the scary bits and get to the end of the novel.

186

Did you hear about what happened to the man who was so scared of life that he took to his bed, believing that he was safe there? He was killed by a broken spring in his mattress!

187

There is no place in the world that is absolutely safe. Believing that you need to be absolutely safe is what keeps you anxious.

188

When you feel anxious, you have basically two options: to go forward and confront what you are scared of, or go backwards and avoid it. Which of these two options is more comfortable and which is likely to lead you to overcome your anxiety? The answers to these two questions are different.

So, if you want to overcome anxiety, accept that the best way to do so is to go forward and confront threat. This will be the more uncomfortable of the two options, but only in the short term.

190

In the early 1980s, I applied for 54 jobs and got none of them. People said, 'How depressing for you', but they were wrong. For I experienced 54 job rejections and zero self-rejections.

191

When you lose something important to you, it's healthy to feel sad.

192

Trying to solve a problem when you are depressed is like walking up a steep hill with both feet tied together.

193

Dealing healthily with unfairness and injustice is one of the most difficult things to cope with. So don't make it any harder by demanding that, because you don't deserve it, unfairness or injustice absolutely must not happen to you. Rather, acknowledge that you are not immune from such unfairness or injustice, no matter how undeserving you are and that you do not have to have such immunity. This will help you to focus on righting the wrong.

194

When you feel sorry for yourself, you believe (1) that you do not deserve to be treated badly and (2) that you absolutely should not be treated in such an undeserving fashion. The problem is with (2) not (1).

195

You keep your feelings of self-pity alive by telling people how terrible it is that you have been treated so badly and by them agreeing with you. So, if you want to tell others about your plight, do *not* agree with them that (a) you absolutely should not have been treated so badly and (b) it is terrible that this happened.

196

---◆---

When others treat you badly and you do not deserve such treatment, recognise that their behaviour is governed by what is in their heads rather than by what you deserve.

197

The first step to overcoming self-pity is to stop feeling ashamed of feeling sorry for yourself.

The next step to overcoming self-pity involves swallowing a bitter pill. It means fully accepting that while you do not deserve to be treated badly, there is no earthly reason why you must be exempt from such bad treatment.

199

Imagine that you are a refugee in a refugee camp. Would you want to be helped by an aid worker who is affected by, but not terribly depressed about, your plight, or by one who is very depressed about what is happening to you?

You would probably want to be helped by the former rather than the latter. Why? Because the aid worker who is terribly depressed won't be able to aid you efficiently. This explains why other-pity is unproductive to both the person pitying and the person being pitied.

If you want to overcome guilt you first need to understand what leads to this emotion. Guilt stems in part from the inference that:

- I have done the wrong thing (sin of commission)
- I have failed to do the right thing (sin of omission)
- I have harmed someone or hurt their feelings.

But guilt really comes from the rigid and extreme attitudes that you hold towards these inferences. Namely:

- I must not do the wrong thing. I am a bad person if I do what I absolutely should not have done.
- I must do the right thing. I am a bad person if I don't do what I absolutely should have done.
- I must not harm another or hurt their feelings. I am a bad person if I harm someone or hurt their feelings.

Remorse is the healthy alternative to guilt. In remorse you make the same inferences as in guilt, namely:

- ➤ I have done the wrong thing (sin of commission)
- ➤ I have failed to do the right thing (sin of omission)
- ➤ I have harmed someone or hurt their feelings.

But when you feel remorse, you hold a different set of attitudes than when you feel guilt. These attitudes are flexible and non-extreme in nature. Namely:

- I wish I hadn't done the wrong thing, but there's no reason why I absolutely should not have done it. I am a fallible human being who did the wrong thing. I am not a bad person.
- I wish I had done the right thing, but there's no reason why I absolutely should have done it. I am a fallible human being who failed to do the right thing. I am not a bad person.
- I wish I had not harmed the other person or hurt their feelings, but there's no reason why I absolutely should not have done so. I am a fallible human being for doing so. I am not a bad person.

Guilt   = responsibility + self-blame
Remorse = responsibility + unconditional self-acceptance

Guilt is the enemy of understanding. When you are feeling guilt as opposed to remorse, you condemn yourself as a bad person. This attitude prevents you from reflecting on and understanding your actions. Since you fail to understand why you acted in the way you did, you are likely to act in a similar way again. Thus, guilt increases rather than decreases the likelihood of future wrong-doing.

204

Remorse promotes understanding. When you are feeling remorse as opposed to guilt, you accept yourself unconditionally as a fallible human being. This attitude encourages you to reflect on and understand your actions. Since you understand why you acted in the way you did, you are less likely to act in a similar way again. Thus, remorse decreases rather than increases the likelihood of future wrong-doing.

205

If you consider that you have to feel guilty about a wrong-doing or else you are in danger of becoming psychopathic, you are mistaken. Remorse is not only a healthy alternative to guilt, it also prevents psychopathy.

Other people can't make you feel guilty. They only issue you with an invitation for you to make yourself feel guilty. Don't accept this invitation, but do take responsibility for any wrong-doing you may have done.

Strictly speaking you don't hurt other people's feelings. They hurt their own feelings about the way you treat them. However, this is NOT an excuse for you to act badly, since you are responsible for the way you behave.

208

Are you a parent who in your heart of hearts does not love one of your children? Or are you a son or daughter who does not love one or both of your parents? Don't feel guilty. There's no law of the universe that states that you must feel that love. If you accept yourself unconditionally for your lack of these loving feelings, you may be able to identify the reason and do something about it. Condemning yourself will only give you an additional problem. You end up by not loving the other person and hating yourself.

When you feel guilty, you focus on your 'sin' and you don't put your behaviour in a wider context. However, when you feel remorseful about your 'sin' you are able to stand back and place your behaviour in such a context.

210

---◆---

When you feel guilty about hurting someone's feelings, you are preoccupied with your own badness rather than concerned with how the other person feels.

211

When you feel guilty, you are preoccupied with the rigid attitude that you absolutely should have known then what you know now. But how could you have known this? Do you have a time machine?

212

Most people think the only alternative to selfishness is selflessness. However, the healthy alternative to both is enlightened self-interest, also known as self-care.

213

Enlightened self-interest involves you primarily looking after yourself, but also involves you looking after the interests of others. Self-care is flexible, and some of the time you will put others' interests before your own.

214

In unhealthy jealousy you are desperate for your partner to reassure you that there is no threat to your relationship. The only problem is that you cannot convince yourself that such reassurance is truly meant if it is given.

215

Unhealthy jealousy is a sure sign of insecurity and low self-esteem. It does not necessarily mean that you are about to lose your loved one.

So, the best way to overcome unhealthy jealousy is for you to give up your need for certainty and to accept yourself unconditionally, whether your partner stays with you or not.

217

---◆---

There are two types of envy: unhealthy envy and healthy envy. Unhealthy envy leads you to attempt to ruin the reputation of those whom you envy. This is *not* a feature of healthy envy, where you are more likely to learn from the person you envy.

Unhealthy envy is based on the rigid attitude that you must have what another has if you don't have it. And if you can't have it, you have to spoil things for the other person.

219

Healthy envy is based on the flexible attitude that you would like to have what another has, but you don't have to have it. Thus, you don't have the motivation to spoil things for others if you can't get what they have.

---◆---

People often confuse envy and jealousy. In jealousy you are preoccupied with losing your partner to another, while in envy you are preoccupied with not having what another person has.

A major obstacle to overcoming unhealthy envy is shame about feeling this way.

222

Why do we like to bring down our heroes and heroines? Because we harbour feelings of unhealthy envy towards them.

223

People who feel unhealthy envy are dangerous to have as enemies.

224

When you feel unhealthy envy, you hold the extreme attitude that gaining something you don't have that another does have will raise your self-esteem if you have it. It will, but only fleetingly.

So, the best way to overcome unhealthy envy is to accept yourself unconditionally when you don't have something that you value which another person has.

---◆---

In a phrase, your worth is not based on what you have or what you lack. If it is based on anything, it is based on your fallibility, your aliveness and your uniqueness.

227

The essence of shame is believing that you are defective, diminished or disgraceful as a person in your entirety.

One of the main differences between shame and guilt lies in your experience of yourself in terms of size and power. In guilt, you often experience yourself as a big, powerful, bad person who has harmed or hurt others. In shame, you often experience yourself as a small, insignificant worm who hopes to disappear entirely from public view.

229

---◆---

Another major difference between shame and guilt concerns what you fear. In shame you fear exclusion from the social group when, whereas in guilt you fear that your social group will be other sinners in hell.

———◆———

Shame is a major reason why people don't deal with their emotional problems. Feeling ashamed about having an emotional problem means that you are more likely to push the issue away than to deal with it.

Some people feel ashamed about feeling ashamed. You can even feel ashamed about your shame about your shame! As human beings, we are often very creative in the way that we deepen our disturbances.

232

Accepting yourself unconditionally as a complex, unrateable, unique human being with strengths, weaknesses and neutral aspects is thus the best antidote to shame that there is.

———◆———

Do you think unwanted thoughts? If so, don't try to stop them. Trying not to think about something will only increase these thoughts. Instead, give up your rigid attitude that you must not have these thoughts and then let them go of their own accord.

———————◆———————

Do you fear losing self-control? If so, it is likely that you are ashamed of doing so. Shame is based on the rigid attitude that you must be in control of yourself at all times and if not, you are a weak person.

The healthy alternative is to develop the flexible attitude that, while perfect personal control may be desirable, it is neither necessary nor possible. When you hold this attitude and you begin to lose control, you will view this as evidence that you are an ordinary human being and not a weak person.

This anti-shame attitude will lead you to feel unanxiously concerned about losing self-control, but not panicked about doing so.

235

Seeking reassurance once or twice over something is fine. But if you are not reassured it is futile to keep seeking reassurance, since you are not reassurable.

236

---◆---

If you seek reassurance compulsively, look for the rigid attitude that underpins your behaviour. It is likely to be: 'I must be certain right now that nothing bad is happening (or is likely to happen) to me.' It is important to change this attitude to: 'I would like to have such certainty, but I don't need it, nor can I get it.' Then it is important to act in a way that is consistent with this attitude. Giving up the dire need for certainty will allow you to live healthily in an uncertain world.

A donkey was dying of thirst in the desert and came to a fork in the road. It knew that one path led to clear water while the other led to dank water that would save its life but make it ill. But the donkey did not know which path led to which type of water. The donkey died. Why? Because it held the rigid attitude that it had to know which road led to the clear water before it set out.

238

———————————◆———————————

When you are indecisive and finally make a decision, you automatically tend to think that your decision is wrong and that the other option which you decided against would have been correct. You tend to think in this way no matter what course of action you finally decide on.

239

Once you have made a decision, it is no good demanding that you absolutely should have done something different, for you empirically should have done exactly what you did. If you accept this, you will move forward. If you don't accept it, you will be stuck in the past.

240

If you think about it, it is not possible to be indecisive. Because when you do nothing, you are actively deciding to do nothing.

241

Some people are anything but indecisive. They are impulsive in their decision-making. They see an attractive option and immediately decide to go for it. When you are indecisive, you hold the rigid attitude that you must not make a mistake but are convinced that you will. When you are impulsive, you hold the rigid attitude that you must have what you want right now and are convinced that you are doing the right thing.

---◆---

When you are indecisive you think too much whereas when you are impulsive in your decision-making you think too little.

243

There are two mistakes that you can make in a leap year (or any other year). You can leap without looking or look without leaping.

The healthy approach is to take care while you look, and then make the leap uncomfortably and accept yourself unconditionally if things don't turn out right.

244

To make a sound decision, it is important that you are in an emotionally good frame of mind. Otherwise, your disturbed emotions will cloud your judgement.

———◆———

Once you are in a good frame of mind, what do you need to do to increase the chances that you will make a sound decision? I suggest the following. Consider the pros and cons of your different options from both a short-term and a long-term perspective as they relate to yourself (and your values in particular) and to relevant others. If you do this rigorously (rather than rigidly!), your preferred option will in all probability, become much clearer to you.

246

Don't wait for inspiration to come before you do something. Do something and inspiration may come. Do nothing and it's unlikely to.

Have you ever said that you couldn't help yourself when you ate that cream cake which spoiled your diet? Of course you couldn't help yourself. After all, the cream cake literally rose off the plate on its own, prised your lips apart and rammed itself down your throat.

Or perhaps it would be wise to take responsibility for your actions instead. Either that or beware low-flying cream cakes!

———————◆———————

Eating, drinking or spending to avoid disturbed feelings won't help you to deal with these feelings. However, doing so may help to set the foundations for an addiction.

249

I do a brisk walk for 50 minutes six mornings a week, and frequently I don't want to do it. But I walk anyway. Why? Because it helps me to stay fit in the long term.

250

Giving up smoking does not involve the application of will power. It involves the application of won't power and following a number of simple steps.

251

The first step to giving up smoking is to be very clear with yourself about why you want to give up. Remind yourself of your goal every time you experience an urge to light up.

252

The second step is to stop buying cigarettes. It's amazing how many people violate this simple rule.

253

The third step is not to accept cigarettes when they are offered to you.

The fourth step involves tolerating the discomfort that you experience when you say no to yourself when you crave a cigarette.

The fifth step involves seeking out and spending time in non-smoking areas and spending time with people who don't smoke. Then, when you feel stronger, gradually expose yourself to smoking environments and don't smoke in them.

256

Make sure that you have the full attention of the other person before you assert yourself with him/her.

257

Once you have learned to assert yourself, you have acquired a very valuable tool. But, don't think that everyone with whom you assert yourself, will listen attentively to you and give you your just desserts. Some will, but others won't. So, if you believe that people have to take you seriously when you assert yourself, you will disturb yourself when they don't. Rather, cultivate the flexible attitude that it would be nice if others took you seriously when you asserted yourself, but they are not obligated to do so.

258

Asserting yourself is healthy, but it doesn't mean that you will get what you want, no matter how skilfully you do it.

259

There are many situations to complain about. If you let them all go you will tend to feel powerless, and if you complain about them all you will tend to feel angry and exhausted. Be selective, and when you have made your choice, be persistent, firm and fight fair.

260

You get the behaviour from others that you are prepared to tolerate from them without protest.

261

When you do something kind for others, most of them will do something kind for you. However, others will exploit your kindness. Don't hold the rigid attitude that everyone must reciprocate your behaviour, because they won't.

262

When people reciprocate your kindness, continue being kind to them. When they take advantage of your kindness, stop being kind to them.

263

If you want someone to listen to you, listen to them first.

264

You cannot change others, but you can influence them to change themselves.

265

However, accept the grim reality that they will often decide not to change.

266

People will often pay more attention to your behaviour than to your words.

267

It is not a good idea to treat all people the same because all people are not the same.

268

People will be who they are, not who you demand them to be.

269

If you want people to respect you, show them by your behaviour that you respect yourself.

270

Other people's emotional problems will often interfere with their ability to listen to reason.

271

If you want to gauge a person's real attitude, watch their behaviour, don't just listen to their words.

272

People often spend too much time trying to change others and not enough time trying to change themselves.

273

If you show others respect then they will show you respect. But not always.

If you want someone to change their behaviour towards you, change your behaviour towards them first.

When you argue with someone you probably hold the rigid attitude that the other person has to see things from your point of view. When you flexibly allow the person in your mind to see things from their point of view and not yours, you are less likely to argue with them.

276

If you hold the rigid attitude that you must have approval from people and are prepared to change yourself to get it, don't be surprised if you end up not knowing who you are.

If you ever became perfect, you would be lonely. Why? Because we tend to shy away from having a relationship with someone without any imperfections. Who wants to be reminded at every turn of how imperfect we are?

278

Treat people as though they are bad and you will increase the chances that they will act badly.

—◆—

If you only listen to others and not to yourself, then you may feel comfortable but you will be out of step with yourself. If you only listen to yourself and not to others, then you will be clear but be out of step with others. But if you listen to yourself *and* to others, you will be in step with yourself and with others.

280

Trying to influence someone for their own good may not be for their own good.

281

Honour your commitments to others and they will tend to honour their commitments to you. Note the word 'tend' here. For some people will not respond in kind.

282

Showing that you understand someone from their standpoint is good for both of you and for your relationship.

If you want to understand someone's behaviour, try to figure out what the person was attempting to achieve by it.

If you hold the rigid attitude that you need to help people, you will probably have relationships with people who need to be helped. If you help them to stand on their own two feet, then expect them to leave you because they don't need you any more.

285

If someone treats you badly, show them that you will not put up with being treated in this way and demonstrate this immediately. The longer you wait, the more likely it is that the other person will continue to treat you badly.

If you don't look after yourself, who will? Only someone who holds the rigid attitude that they need to look after people, and you won't want a relationship with such a person in the long term.

287

Having a relationship with a person who holds the rigid attitude that they need you is ultimately unhealthy for both of you.

Showing your loved ones that you accept them warts and all and that you want them to be themselves is one of the two main keys to excellent relationships. Encouraging them to do the same for you is the other key.

289

Love does not mean putting up with bad behaviour from those you love.

---◆---

People who hold the rigid attitude that they need people are the unluckiest people in the world. Why? Because of their neediness.

291

People who hold the flexible attitude that they very much prefer to have people in their life but do not need them are the healthiest people in the world.

292

If you hold the rigid attitude that you need to be needed, you cannot have a healthy relationship because you will tend be only involved with those who are psychologically immature.

293

When we show others that we can be vulnerable, most of them will be prepared to show us their vulnerabilities. But others, a minority fortunately, will seek to exploit our vulnerabilities for their own disturbed gains.

If someone with whom you want a relationship does not want a relationship with you, that is both bad and good. It's bad because your desire will not be fulfilled, but it's good because you won't waste time trying to develop a relationship with someone who is not for you.

295

If someone does not want a relationship with you, let them go. Trying to get them to change their mind will only sour relations between the two of you.

296

Being dependent upon someone means not using your own resources.

If you only give in a relationship, you will probably end up resenting the fact that the other person only takes. Don't be resentful, since without realising it you have trained the other person to expect to take from you and not to give back.

298

If you only take in a relationship, you will probably end up being alone.

299

A healthy relationship is marked by a willingness of both people to give and to receive.

300

If you allow others to dominate you, most will.

If you cannot be at ease with yourself when you are by yourself, then you will find it difficult to be at ease with others, for holding the rigid attitude that you need to be with others to avoid the horrors of being alone will make you scared that they will leave you. Overcoming the horrors of being alone will help you be at ease with others and by yourself.

———◆———

There are times when to follow the maxim: 'when it feels good, do it' is definitely a good idea and there are times when doing so is definitely a bad idea. Thinking of your long-term healthy interests will help you to decide which is which.

303

If you are going to tackle your procrastination, start today.

304

There are four basic reasons why people procrastinate on tasks that are in their best interests to do:

- Fear of failure;
- Fear of disappointing others;
- Fear of discomfort;
- Rebellion.

305

---◆---

Putting off doing something that is it not in your best interests to do is not procrastination. It is sensible.

306

People often ask me how I manage to write so much. The answer is discipline. When I am in a writing phase, I resolve to write 500 words a day every day. 'But,' they ask, 'what if you are not in the mood?' My answer is this: 'If I'm not in the mood, I start writing anyway, and nine times out of ten I get in the mood.' So, if you want to do something and are not in the mood, don't let that stop you. Begin anyway.

Chances are that, like me, you'll soon get into the mood. You don't need to be in the mood to do something.

307

If you wait until you feel like doing something onerous that is in your best interests to do, you will wait too long.

308

Avoiding things will not usually help you to solve your problems. But, if you really want to avoid something, make sure you avoid your avoidance.

309

Persistence is a virtue if the activity you are persisting with helps you to achieve your goals. However, persisting with an activity that does not enhance good achievement is counterproductive.

It is said that humans have descended from the ape, but most of us are descendants of the ostrich, so strong is our tendency to bury our heads in the sand and not face up to dealing with painful issues.

311

Discipline involves you doing something that you don't want to do in order to get the results that you do want.

312

You are not lazy, but you may hold the extreme attitude that it's too hard to do something that is unpleasant but worth doing. You can change this attitude more easily than you could change your supposed inherent laziness.

Lists are fine if they promote constructive action.

314

If you leave things until the last minute, you may motivate yourself but in an unduly pressurised way.

315

Just because your parents are your parents, it doesn't follow that they have to love you. Why? Because your parents are human first and your parents second and being human means that their emotional problems may interfere with them loving you.

316

Also, for the same reasons, there is no law of the universe which decrees that you have to love your parents.

317

Your parents influence you as you grow up and teach you various standards. But you bring your own rigid attitude to those standards and it is this rigidity, not your failure to live up to those standards, which are at the core of your emotional problems.

318

If your parents mistreated you, they probably did so because of their own emotional problems. This is not meant to excuse your parents but to help you to understand why they may have acted in the way that they did.

319

Your parents may say that you will always be their little boy or little girl. But this does not mean that you have to act like one with them.

320

The only way to prove to your parents that you are an adult is to act like an adult with them and to do so consistently. After a while, they'll probably get the message.

321

However, some parents never get the message.

322

If they don't, remember that they will view you in the way they choose to view you and not in the way that you want to be viewed.

Encourage your adult children to do what is in their best interests, not what is in yours. But who decides what is in their best interests? If you think that you do, then you have a problem letting your adult children be adults.

———◆———

Parents who show their children that they respect themselves and that they have time for themselves as well as time for their children serve as good role models for their children.

325

Parents who put themselves last all the time, and who show their children that they don't have time for themselves and only time for their children, serve as poor role models and doormats for their children.

326

You didn't choose your biological parents. But remember, your biological parents didn't choose you, either.

327

Insisting that you are nothing like your parents will lead you to over-emphasise your similarity with them.

328

People often complain about the simplicity of the ideas expressed in this book. They are simple, but they are difficult to apply. Simple doesn't mean easy.

329

It is important that you understand the difference between intellectual insight and emotional insight if your personal change is to be meaningful.

———◆———

Intellectual insight involves seeing that something makes sense but only having a slight conviction in it. This type of insight is not sufficient to lead to meaningful emotional and behavioural change. It is summed up in statements such as, 'I can see it in my head, but I don't feel it in my gut.'

331

Emotional insight involves seeing that something makes sense and having a strong conviction in it. This type of insight does lead to meaningful emotional and behavioural change. It is summed up in statements such as, 'I both see it in my head and feel it in my gut.'

332

Meaningful personal change therefore involves moving from intellectual insight to emotional insight. This is easier said than done but the good news is that you can make the journey.

333

However, most people won't make this journey because they hold the extreme attitude that it is too hard. The journey is hard, but in reality it isn't *too* hard.

Others won't make the journey because they hold the rigid attitude that they absolutely shouldn't have to make the journey and that they must get emotional insight immediately and if they don't then they won't work towards achieving it.

335

It is important that you acknowledge that personal change involves feeling uncomfortable. Holding the rigid attitude that you must be comfortable while you change is a sure way of stopping yourself from changing.

336

---◆---

When you commit yourself to personal change, it is important to realise that sometimes you will take two steps forward and one step back, and at other times you will take one step forward and two steps back.

The important thing is to learn from your setbacks and keep moving forward.

337

An important part of a personal change programme involves you weakening your conviction in your rigid and extreme attitudes and strengthening your conviction in your flexible and non-extreme attitudes.

338

But perhaps the most important part of a personal change programme is acting on your newly acquired flexible and non-extreme attitudes. Unless you act on these attitudes, you will not internalise them and they will not make a difference to your everyday life.

339

One of the best ways to strengthen your conviction in a flexible and non-extreme attitude that makes sense to you and you wish to adopt is to act *as if* you already hold it.

———◆———

How much time do you spend every day maintaining your physical well-being? You'd be surprised how much time you spend on washing yourself, cleaning yourself, feeding yourself, and on exercising, etc.

If you were to spend half this time every day maintaining your psychological well-being, you would be pleasantly surprised at the difference this would make to your life.

341

Changing unwanted personal habits takes hard work and persistence. If anyone tells you otherwise and promises you a quick and easy way to achieve your goals, they probably want to get rich at your expense.

When you begin to change, it won't feel natural. It's not supposed to. So, as you change accept the fact that you won't feel like yourself for a while.

It is important to distinguish between feeling better and getting better. Feeling better without getting better involves a temporary distraction from what you are disturbed about. Getting better and not feeling better occurs when you begin to address your emotional problems in a constructive way, a process which is painful. Getting better and feeling better occurs when you have successfully overcome your problems.

344

Most people want to feel better more than to get better because they want a painless solution to their emotional problems which largely does not exist.

345

So, if you want to get better realise that this involves you bearing a period of not feeling better, and in some cases a period of feeling worse, as you confront and deal with painful issues that you may have partly avoided.

———◆———

In order to change, it is important to acknowledge that this involves you regularly changing the way you behave and the way that you think *before* your feelings begin to change. Feelings are slow starters when it comes to the change process.

If you are going to change, it is vital that your actions are consistent with your flexible and non-extreme attitudes. It is no good thinking one way and acting in a way that is inconsistent with these attitudes. You will just undermine the change process if you do so.

348

Change involves noticing small signs of progress and building on them.

349

Ignoring small signs of progress and focusing on the gap between where you are and where you want to be will block your progress.

350

Do you hold the rigid attitude that personal changes be quick, painless and effortless? Then you won't change at all.

351

Half-hearted action will yield moderate results.

352

Committed action will yield far better results.

353

Practice makes better, not perfect.

Thought without action may be interesting, but it is theoretical. Action without thought may be exciting but it is potentially dangerous. Thoughtful action is the best of both worlds.

355

'I'll try,' comes before 'I didn't.'

356

Trying to do something is far less effective than doing it.

357

Confidence comes from doing things unconfidently.

358

Here are three approaches to personal change. Which approach would you choose?

Approach 1: Opting to feel better but getting worse

Approach 2: Opting to feel worse before getting better

Approach 3: Opting to feel better before getting better

Number 2 is the only realistic approach to personal change. If you opt for number 3 you will have a very long wait.

359

If something seems too difficult, break it down into smaller steps.

If at first you don't succeed, try the same thing twice more. Then consider the possibility that what you are doing won't yield the results that you are striving for.

361

Working hard at something strengthens your psychological muscles for working hard.

362

Reading self-help books won't help you to solve your problems. Repeatedly putting into practice what you read in such books may do so.

363

Don't follow maxims slavishly and unthinkingly – even this one.

364

---◆---

A defining feature of psychological health is being able to think for yourself. Thus, I would be happier for you to think critically about what I have written in this book and to conclude that I am wrong than I would be for you to accept uncritically what I have written as being correct.

365

Compile and review a quote book of your own containing maxims that you find particularly helpful and inspiring.

366

If you've enjoyed this book, tell your friends. If you haven't tell me... Oh, you can also tell me that you've enjoyed it if you want to!

www.ingramcontent.com/pod-product-compliance
Lightning Source LLC
Chambersburg PA
CBHW071220290326
41931CB00037B/1485